CONTINENTS

Europe

Leila Merrell Foster

Heinemann LIBRARY

www.heinemann.co.uk/library
Visit our website to find out more information about Heinemann Library books.

To order:

Phone ++44 (0)1865 888066
Send a fax to ++44 (0)1865 314091
Visit the Heinemann Bookshop at www.heinemann.co.uk/library to browse our catalogue and
order online.

First published in Great Britain by Heinemann Library,
Halley Court, Jordan Hill, Oxford OX2 8EJ, a division of
Reed Educational and Professional Publishing Ltd.
Heinemann is a registered trademark of Reed Educational
and Professional Publishing Ltd.

OXFORD MELBOURNE AUCKLAND JOHANNESBURG
BLANTYRE GABORONE IBADAN PORTSMOUTH NH (USA)
CHICAGO

Designed by Depke Design
Originated by Dot Gradations
Printed by South China Printing in Hong Kong, China

06 05 04 03 02
10 9 8 7 6 5 4 3 2 1
ISBN 0 431 15790 1

British Library Cataloguing in Publication Data
Foster, Leila Merrell
    Europe. – (Continents)
    1.Europe – Juvenile literature
    I.Title
    914

Acknowledgements
The Publishers would like to thank the following for
permission to reproduce copyright material:
Bruce Coleman, Inc./Lee Foster, p. 5; Earth Scenes/P.
O'Toole, p. 7; Photo Edit/Tony Freeman, p. 9; Tony
Stone/Shaun Egan, p. 11; Bruce Coleman, Inc./Olivier
Lequeinec, p. 13; Animals Animals/Darek Karp, p. 14; Bruce
Coleman, Inc./Wedlgo Ferchland, p. 15; Corbis/Tony Arruza,
p. 16; Tony Stone/Michael Busselle, p. 17; Photo Edit/Amy
Etra, p. 19; Bruce Coleman, Inc./Masha Nor dbye, p. 20;
Tony Stone/John Lamb, p. 21; Bruce Coleman, Inc./Guido
Cozzi, pp. 22, 25; Bruce Coleman, Inc./C. & J. McClurg, p. 24;
Tony Stone/Arnold Husmo, p. 26; Bruce Coleman, Inc., p. 27;
Photo Edit/Bill Buchmann, p. 28.

Cover photo reproduced with permission of Science Photo
Library/Tom Van Sant, Geosphere Project/Planetary Visions.

Our thanks to Jane Bingham for her assistance in the
preparation of this book.

Every effort has been made to contact copyright holders
of any material reproduced in this book. Any omissions
will be rectified in subsequent printings if notice is given
to the Publisher.

Contents

Some words are shown in bold, **like this.**
You can find out what they mean by looking in the glossary.

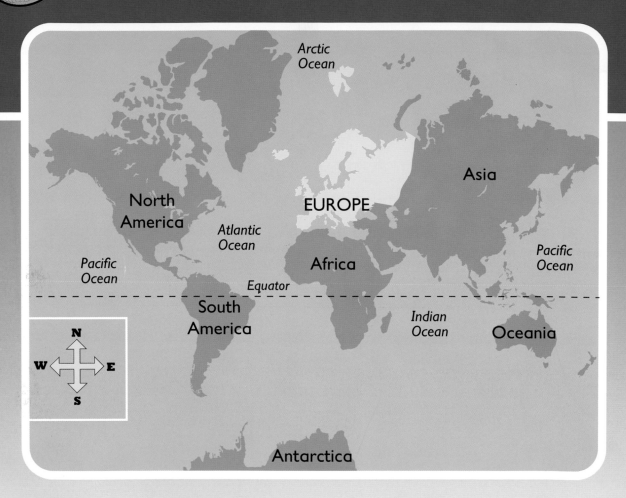

Arctic
Ocean

Asia

North
America

EUROPE

Atlantic
Ocean

Pacific
Ocean

Africa

Pacific
Ocean

Equator

South
America

Indian
Ocean

Oceania

N

W ← → E

S

Antarctica

A continent is a vast mass of land that covers part
of the Earth's surface. There are seven continents in the
world, and Europe is the second smallest. To the north
of Europe is the icy Arctic Ocean. To the west is the
Atlantic Ocean. The warm Mediterranean Sea lies
between southern Europe and Africa.

Islands off the coast of Norway

The continent of Europe includes many islands. Most of these are very small and belong to larger countries, but some are **independent** nations. The island of Iceland, in the far north of the Atlantic Ocean, is a country in its own right. To the east of Europe is the much larger continent of Asia.

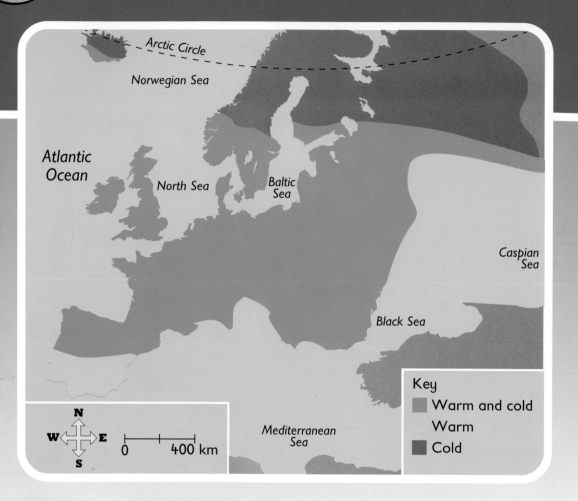

- Arctic Circle
- Norwegian Sea
- Atlantic Ocean
- North Sea
- Baltic Sea
- Caspian Sea
- Black Sea
- Mediterranean Sea

N
W E
S
0   400 km

Key
- Warm and cold
- Warm
- Cold

Europe has many different **climates**. Some parts of Europe lie north of the **Arctic Circle**. They are covered in ice all the year round. Countries in the south, around the Mediterranean Sea, have a much warmer climate. The weather in the south of Europe is warm and wet in winter and hot and dry in summer.

Misty weather in Scotland

Countries in Western Europe have a mild (warm) climate, with lots of rain and mist. These countries do not get very cold in winter or very hot in summer. Warm **currents** in the Atlantic Ocean stop the coasts of western Europe from becoming icy.

Mountains

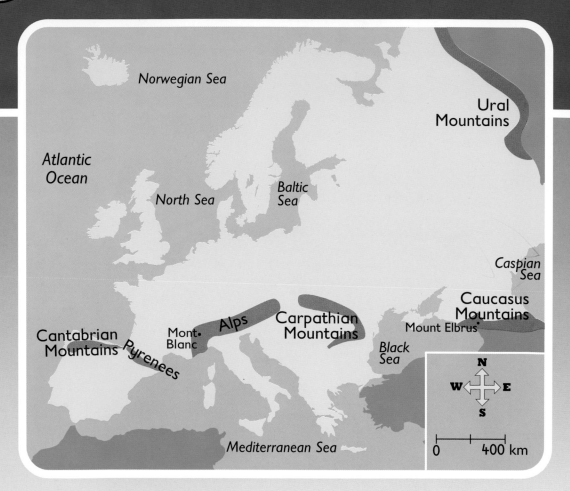

Norwegian Sea

Ural Mountains

Atlantic Ocean

North Sea

Baltic Sea

Caspian Sea

Caucasus Mountains

Cantabrian Mountains

Mont. Blanc

Alps

Pyrenees

Carpathian Mountains

Mount Elbrus

Black Sea

N
W E
S

0   400 km

Mediterranean Sea

Europe is crossed by many high mountain **ranges**. To the east are the Urals, a line of snow-capped peaks that separate Europe from the continent of Asia. The Caucasus Mountains, in the south, also form a **border** with Asia. Mount Elbrus in the Caucasus Mountains is the highest peak in Europe.

Jungfrau peak, the Swiss Alps

The Alps stretch for over 1000 kilometres across Southern Europe. They run through five different countries – France, Italy, Switzerland, Austria and Yugoslavia. The highest mountain is the Alps is Mont Blanc. There is a long tunnel underneath it so that cars can cross the Alps more easily.

 Rivers

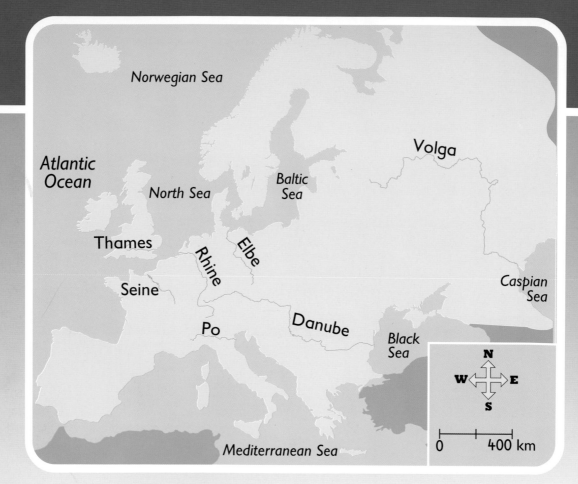

The longest river in Europe is the Volga. It flows through Russia for 3530 kilometres, but it is usually frozen for three months each year. The River Rhine runs through the Netherlands, Germany and Switzerland. It is linked by a canal to the River Danube. This means that ships can travel right across Europe.

River Danube, Budapest, Hungary

Europe's second longest river is the Danube. It flows through nine European countries. Ships and **barges** carry people and goods to cities on the Danube. The **capital cities** of Vienna, Budapest and Belgrade are all on the River Danube.

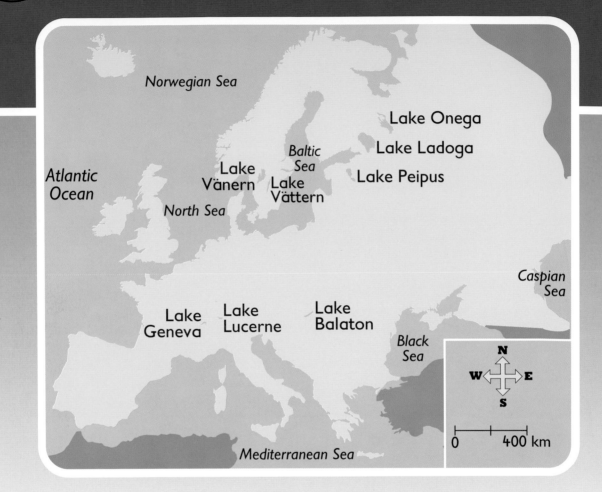

Europe has many large **freshwater** lakes. The largest is Lake Ladoga in Russia. Lake Ladoga used to be filled with fish, but now some of these fish are dying because the lake is **polluted**. Many lakes and rivers in Europe have been polluted by chemical waste from factories or by **pesticides** from farms.

Boats on Lake Geneva, Switzerland

Switzerland has many beautiful lakes, like Lake Geneva and Lake Lucerne. People often use these lakes for sailing and windsurfing. Some of Europe's lakes provide water for people to use in their homes. The water flows through a special **water treatment plant** that makes it safe to drink.

Animals

Grey wolf in Poland

Many wild animals that used to live in Europe have almost disappeared. People have hunted wolves and bears for hundreds of years. Now these animals are very rare and only live in **remote** mountains and forests. However, many deer and foxes live in the wild in Europe.

Reindeer herd in Sweden

In the far north of Europe, people catch reindeer and keep them in herds. The reindeer are kept for their milk, meat and fur. Other animals that live in the icy north are polar bears, whales and seals. In the warm south, there are lizards and snakes.

Plants

Olive trees in Spain

Many farmers in Italy, Greece and Spain grow olive trees. The fruit of the olive tree can be eaten whole or crushed to make cooking oil. Orange and lemon trees also grow in these warm southern countries. In the Netherlands, where it is cooler, people grow fields of colourful tulips.

Vineyard in the Loire, France

Europe is famous for its grapes that are crushed to make wine. Grape vines are planted in fields called vineyards. Most vineyards are in southern Europe, where the grapes get plenty of sun. In northern Europe there are thick forests of evergreen trees, such as pines.

Countries

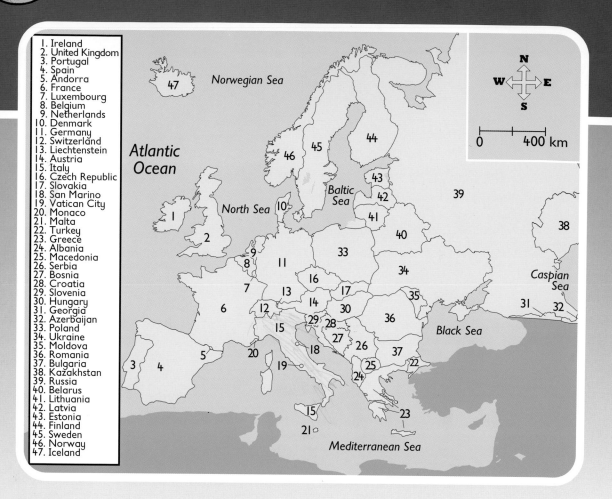

1. Ireland
2. United Kingdom
3. Portugal
4. Spain
5. Andorra
6. France
7. Luxembourg
8. Belgium
9. Netherlands
10. Denmark
11. Germany
12. Switzerland
13. Liechtenstein
14. Austria
15. Italy
16. Czech Republic
17. Slovakia
18. San Marino
19. Vatican City
20. Monaco
21. Malta
22. Turkey
23. Greece
24. Albania
25. Macedonia
26. Serbia
27. Bosnia
28. Croatia
29. Slovenia
30. Hungary
31. Georgia
32. Azerbaijan
33. Poland
34. Ukraine
35. Moldova
36. Romania
37. Bulgaria
38. Kazakhstan
39. Russia
40. Belarus
41. Lithuania
42. Latvia
43. Estonia
44. Finland
45. Sweden
46. Norway
47. Iceland

Norwegian Sea

Atlantic Ocean

North Sea

Baltic Sea

Caspian Sea

Black Sea

Mediterranean Sea

There are over 47 countries in Europe. By far the largest is Russia and the smallest is the Vatican City. Russia is made up of many different **regions**. It is partly in Europe and partly in Asia. The Vatican City is the home of the **Pope**. The whole country takes up less than half a square kilometre!

Outdoor news stand in Rome, Italy

Most countries in Europe have their own language, and some countries have more than one language. Altogether, about 60 different languages are spoken in Europe. Some of these languages, such as Russian and Greek, have different letters from the ones used in English.

Cities

Red Square, Moscow

Moscow is the **capital** of Russia. At the heart of Moscow is Red Square. This is where the leaders of Russia work in a group of buildings called the Kremlin. The photograph shows the Kremlin and St Basil's cathedral. The cathedral was built by a cruel but powerful ruler called Ivan the Terrible.

Houses of Parliament, London

London was built by the Ancient Romans and soon grew into a large and important city. For over 700 years, the British **Parliament** has met in the Houses of Parliament on the banks of the River Thames. The famous writer Charles Dickens lived in London. His story *Oliver Twist* is set in the city.

The Parthenon, Athens

The city of Athens was once the centre of Ancient Greece. High above the city, the Greeks built a temple to their goddess of wisdom and war. This temple was called the Parthenon. Now the Parthenon is in ruins, but people still follow the ideas of the great thinkers and leaders of ancient Athens.

This map shows some of the most important cities in Europe. Paris is one of the world's most beautiful cities. It has wide, tree-lined streets called boulevards and fine churches. Paris is also a centre for fashion. Clothes designers from all over the world come to see the Paris fashion collections.

Fishing boats in Portugal

All round the coast of Europe, people go fishing. In the cold northern seas, they catch cod, herring and haddock. Sardines, tuna and shellfish are found in the warmer southern seas. Some fishermen still use small boats, but most fishing is done by huge **trawlers** that drag enormous nets behind them.

Farmhouse in Denmark

All over Europe, farmers grow wheat, which is ground into flour. In northern Europe, the flour is used mainly for bread, and in southern Europe it is often used to make pasta. Northern Europe has many **dairy farms**, where cows produce milk, which is made into cream, butter and cheese.

Troll fjord, Norway

The coast of Norway has hundreds of rocky fjords. These steep-sided channels were cut into the rock by ice millions of years ago. Large ships can sail far inland along the fjords because the water in them is so deep.

The Colosseum, Rome, Italy

The Colosseum was a vast stone stadium that was built by the Ancient Romans almost 2000 years ago. The Roman emperors put on spectacular shows in the Colosseum to keep their people happy. Huge crowds came to watch warriors, called gladiators, fight each other to the death.

Eiffel Tower, Paris, France

The Eiffel Tower was built in 1889 and it is still a famous place to visit. For over 40 years it was the tallest building in the world, until the Empire State Building was put up in New York. Visitors can take a lift or climb up hundreds of stairs to reach the top of the tower.

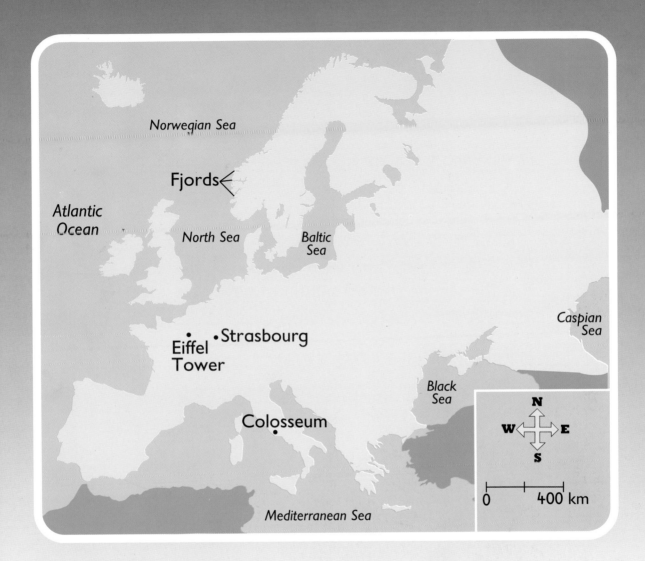

Some European countries have joined a group called the European Union. This is also known as the EU. Members of the EU meet to discuss how the countries of Europe can work together. There is a European **Parliament** at Strasbourg in France, and most EU countries use Euro bank notes and coins.

1. Europe produces more goods than any other continent.

2. The world's largest lake – the Caspian Sea – lies partly in Europe.

3. Europe is the most crowded continent in the world. It is the second smallest continent, but only Asia has more people.

4. More than half the land in Europe is used for farming.

5. Europe has the largest country in the world, Russia, and the world's smallest country, Vatican City.

6. Rotterdam, in the Netherlands, is one of the busiest ports in the world.

7. The Saint Gotthard tunnel in central Switzerland is the world's longest tunnel for motor traffic. It is 16.3 kilometres long.

8. Finland has 55,000 lakes and is known as the 'land of thousands of lakes'.

9. Mount Elbrus in the Caucasus Mountains is the highest peak in Europe. It is 5642 metres high.

Glossary

Arctic Circle imaginary line that circles the Earth near the North Pole

barge large boat with a flat bottom, used to carry heavy loads

border dividing line between one country and another

capital city city where government leaders work

climate kind of weather a place has

current strong movement of water

dairy farm farm where cows or goats are kept for their milk

freshwater water that is not salty

goods things that people buy and use

independent free to govern itself

parliament group of people who make the laws of their country

pesticide chemical used to kill insects

polluted poisoned or damaged by something harmful

Pope the head of the Roman Catholic Church

range line of connected mountains

region large area that often has its own government

remote far away from people

trawler fishing boat that drags a bag-shaped net through the water

water treatment plant place where water is treated with chemicals to make it clean and free from germs

More books to read

An Illustrated Atlas of Europe, Keith Lye, Cherrytree
  Books, 2000

Europe, Ewan McLeish, Hodder Childrens
  Books, 2000

Index